Extreme(ly Dumb) Sports

The Duckboy Guide

No animals were injured in the making of this book. Several, however, are thoroughly embarrassed to have been involved, and wish to remain anonymous.

Extreme(ly Dumb) Sports

The Duckboy Guide

by

Paul Stanton

Drawings
by Mike Gouse

DUCKBOY CARDS INC.

Published by Duckboy Cards Inc., Hamilton MT

Library of Congress Control Number: 2003099527

ISBN 1-883364-16-7

First Printing, March 2004
Printed in U.S.A.

Distributed by Duckboy Cards Inc.
PO Box 2095, Hamilton, Montana 59840, USA
Phone 1-800-761-5741

Distributed to the Book Trade by The Globe Pequot Press, Guilford CT

Please visit our website at http://www.duckboy.com

CONTENTS

Against stupidity the very gods
themselves contend in vain.
—Schiller, *The Maid of Orleans*, III, 6

Stupid is as stupid does.
—Forrest Gump

Acknowledgements

Thanks to the many people courageous enough to appear in my photos. For their expert advice and assistance, thank you to David Horgan and Mountain Press Publishing, both of Missoula Montana.

I thank the Historical Museum at Fort Missoula, Missoula Montana, for allowing me to use their logging locomotive in the pictures on the cover, and on page 89.

For inspiration, I'm indebted to all the towelsnappers out there, who turn to the sports page first. To the extreme sports enthusiasts, especially those who put the "dumb" into *Extreme(ly Dumb) Sports*, thanks for my greatest challenge: creating imaginary sports and situations more outlandish than real life as they live it.

Hang Gliding

INTRODUCTION

Sport is America's greatest source of recreation, broken bones, and bad metaphors. It's also our favorite excuse for aberrant behavior. Normally, if you go around slamming your head into hard objects, you'll be locked in a padded room. But if you call it "soccer," then it's OK. Everyone knows soccer is part of a sinister European plot (along with the Mini Cooper and the metric system) to scramble the brains of American youth, but we excuse it in the name of sport.

We often describe our lives in sports terms. As teenagers, we didn't kiss, we "got to first base." If something is sure, it's a "slam dunk." An unknown candidate is a "dark horse." An unacceptable comment or action is "out of bounds." Something that's mediocre or normal is "par for the course." To get away with something is to "pull an OJ." A tough, unappetizing piece of meat is a "Mike Tyson cutlet."

While many of us think of athletics as the domain of the young and fit, the world of sport is much more comprehensive. Sport includes a spectrum of activities, from skydiving to chess. It allows for apparent contradictions such as the existence of "sports bars".

Indeed, some sports take place mainly in bars, including foosball, darts, inflatable-suit sumo wrestling, and the '80's phenomena of mechanical bull riding and Jello wrestling. These days, if it's dumb enough, it could be a sport.

While dumb sports have been with us forever, in recent years the movement has been towards *Extremely Dumb* Sports. Why do something difficult and dangerous, and come off looking merely silly, when with a little extra effort you can demonstrate transcendent stupidity?

Since 1987 I've been taking photographs for use in postcards and other products. Because many of the photos have dealt with the subject of sports, especially the Extremely Dumb ones, I've collected them in this book to explore the subject. While organized sports can be Extremely Dumb, it requires the freedom and imagination of the individual to really push the envelope. Most of the sports I've included here are the individual, disorganized sports, such as *snowshoe ballet, fishing for sand trout,* and *mobile home snagging.* I hope these photos will convince you that there's at least one Extremely Dumb Sport for everyone.

Water Sports

Sixty percent of the earth's surface is covered by water (another twenty percent by car lots and Starbucks). It's fitting that many of our most popular sports activities are held in Neptune's realm. There are endless varieties of Extremely Dumb water sports.

Scuba diving, a sport invented by Lloyd Bridges, gives participants the chance to view coral reefs, search for sunken treasure, and wrestle giant squid.

"Personal watercraft," such as Waverunners and Jetskis, are aquatic motorcycles. They're the vehicles of choice for motorheads who've become bored with running into things on land. These machines were designed to annoy and frighten swimmers, fishermen, and canoeists. Their secondary function is recreation.

Water skiing requires that you let a fast boat drag you on the end of a rope like a tetherball. The boat is necessary because it's really hard to find a lake with a hill in it. And if you do, the lift lines are really long.

The whole point of whitewater rafting is to take a boat places a boat shouldn't be. It's like a very wet demolition derby. My friends and I once rowed a surplus aircraft carrier life raft down Desolation Canyon in Utah. The *Waterdog*, when loaded, was about the size, shape, and weight of a '56 Buick, and rowing it with 11-foot oars was very good exercise. It didn't handle nearly as well as the Buick, so you had to start pulling in the direction you wanted to go about a half-mile upstream.

Water Polo

Fortunately, we didn't bump into too many large, sharp rocks. Still, we were lucky the Navy built very tough rafts. It floated just as well upside-down as right side up.

Gator Wrestling

There are plenty of minor water sports like water polo ("We drown a lot of horses that way") water ballet, gator wrestling, and gator ballet.

One of the newest minor water sports is called "skipping." It involves a snowmobile, a body of (liquid) water, and, I presume, a lot of beer. The idea is to get a snowmobile up to speed on land, then skip it across the surface of a lake or river to the other bank.

If the snowmobile has enough power, *and it* doesn't hit any obstacle on the water (like a duck feather), *and* if the driver doesn't throttle back or lose his balance, then the machine *may* remain on the surface.

Some states are trying to decide whether to regulate or ban skipping, because of the obvious safety and pollution concerns. My suggestion is to allow this activity, with these requirements:

1. To protect the water from pollution, the fuel tank must be sealed.

2. The operator must be securely chained to the machine.

3. No life jackets.

I know it's a harsh rule, but do you really want to meet someone this Extremely Dumb driving home on the highways?

Swimming is the most basic and important of all water sports. Most aquatic sports, such as diving, sailing, windsurfing and rowing, allow you to get into the water, whether you plan on it or not. Swimming enables you to get back out. Non-swimmers who do water sports aren't Extremely Dumb. They're insane.

DO-IT-YOURSELF DIVING GEAR

Elmo's Discount Guide Service

SPRING MOBILE HOME SNAGGING SEASON

WATERFALL-SKIING: NO SPORT FOR SISSIES

WATER HOCKEY: FINDING THE PUCK IS HALF THE FUN

PLAYING "TIDAL WAVE" WITH UNCLE GUS

IMPROVING THE KIDS' MOTOR SKILLS

The Great Outdoors

My grandfather, who came west walking behind a covered wagon, passed one piece of wisdom down through the family. He'd say, "If I was as smart as you, I wouldn't stay here or anywhere else. I'd just go down to St. Louie and saunter around." To this day, we have no idea what he was talking about.

He did, however, convey his enjoyment of being outdoors. Many of our most enjoyable times are spent under the open sky, feeling the wind in our hair, the good earth under our feet, the sun scorching our hides, and the bugs biting our backsides.

I live in Montana, where nearly everyone enjoys backpacking, camping, or hiking. Backpacking is like *The Grapes of Wrath*, but without the truck.

Camping is like being homeless, but you do it on purpose. Hiking was invented by Moses and became popular during the Crusades. A hike differs from a stroll, an amble, a saunter or a walk, due to its intensity. When you tell someone to "take a hike" you infer that he may never return. All of these sports can test one's woodcraft.

When I was a boy, my father taught me many of the necessary skills for survival in the mountains. He taught me to take enough food and plan my route carefully. "Remember the Donner Party," he'd say. "Pack well, leave early, and travel with a friend—a big, meaty one." He taught me how to build a fire and set up a tent, and which plants will not substitute for toilet paper. Elk thistle, for example, is entirely unsuitable. He taught me, when heating a can of beans on the car exhaust manifold, first punch a small hole in the lid. Otherwise, you'll be eating your beans off the underside of the hood.

19

In the mountains it's important to learn about safety around wild animals. Give moose plenty of room. Don't pat a buffalo on the head. Wear "bear bells" to avoid startling a bear, and carry pepper spray. It's also important to know the difference between grizzly bears and black bears. One way is to identify the scat each species leaves. Folks say grizzly scat has bells in it and smells like pepper spray.

Outdoor sports are so popular in Montana that people move here just to heed the Call of the Wilderness. Others move here to heed the *Voices* in their heads, which command them to move into a cabin in the woods and begin hoarding weapons.

The Great Outdoors is home to many Extremely Dumb Sports. Bicycling has become so popular that each spring brings the "Spandex Hatch". Golf lets grown men wear clothes that would have got them beat up if they had dressed that way as kids. In both tennis and auto racing a few people get to compete, and everyone else sits in the stands, swiveling their heads from side to side.

The dumbest outdoor sport of all is field hockey. I tried this only once, and I spent most of my time pulling my skate blades out of the sod.

Field Hockey

TABLE TENNIS

"Bright out, ain't it?"

PLAYING "KICK THE CAN" WITH DAD

"ROLL OVER, HONEY....YOU'RE SNORING!"

BODY BOWLING

HORIZONTAL BUNGEE JUMPING

HITCHHIKING IN WINDY WYOMING

SEARCHING FOR ENLIGHTENMENT, OR ONE OF ITS SUBURBS

TROPICAL GOLF

ONE OF AMERICA'S TOUGHER GOLF HOLES

HITTING OUT OF THE ROUGH

HILLBILLY STRETCH LIMO

BOULDER SURFING: NOT FOR THE FAINT-HEARTED

Squash Tournament

Working Out

The difference between "working" and "working out" is economic. If someone pays you to move large, heavy objects, that's "working". If you pay someone else to let you move large, heavy objects, that's "working out."

In the good old days people walked everywhere and they had to move heavy loads by hand, whether they wanted to or not. They never considered paying for the privilege: "Give me five chickens, and I'll let you and your friends move this big block of limestone to the top of that pyramid." Back then, the average lifespan was 40 years or so, because nobody knew such hard, brutal work was good for you.

Safety is important when working out, to avoid being crushed, burned, impaled, or otherwise interrupted. When doing bench presses, for example, use a "spotter" to remove the bar from your throat before you stop breathing. Proper clothing is also a safety issue. I knew a guy who died while jogging in Montana. He was a vegetarian, and he wore a T shirt that read "If you love animals, don't eat them." He was run over by a cattle truck.

Exercise is so important to your health that you should do it even if it kills you. Science has shown that, while several hours of hard daily exercise may not make you live longer, it will, without question, make your life *seem* longer. If you pick a sufficiently unpleasant exercise program, and stick to it with grim determination, you'll feel like you're *never* going to die, no matter how badly you may want to.

That's why I drink so much coffee. Some days "the shakes" is the only exercise I get.

MABEL BECOMES FRED'S PERSONAL TRAINER

AEROBIC SNOWMOBILING

WATCHING BEARS CHASE JOGGERS...A GROWING SPECTATOR SPORT

SYLVIA'S SEPTEMBER WORKOUT--
THROWING OUT REFUSE, RECYCLABLES, AND RELATIVES

"Beefaerobics"--The Latest Attempt to Raise Leaner Beef

Arlene's Exercise Bike

Low-Impact Aerobics

BILL'S FIREWOOD PROJECT GETS OUT OF HAND

CLEANING THE POTS AND PANS

"Working Out" in Winter

CALIFORNIA POWER STATION #247 COMES ONLINE

SPRING CYCLING IN MINNESOTA

Critter Sports

A lady walks into a bar with a duck under her arm. An old drunk looks up and says, "Where'd ya get that PIG?" She sniffs, "This is not a pig, it's a duck!" The drunk says, "I was **talkin'** to the duck."

Animals are more than fodder for old jokes. They are an important part of life, and especially the sporting life. Without animals in sports, rodeo cowboys would have to rope and ride each other, which would add a different (and kinky) dimension. It wouldn't be much fun for a college student to teach his roommate to leap into the air and catch a Frisbee in his mouth. Without animals, the Midwest would lose its favorite sport, cow tipping.

Some "animal rights" people think using animals in sport is wrong. I disagree. If PETA had its way, thousands of wrestling alligators in Florida would be out of work. Unemployed sled dogs would be panhandling on the streets of Anchorage. Show cats would be prowling alleys looking for mice. Homing pigeons would join the homeless. And the celebrated jumping frogs of Calaveras County would be on some Frenchman's menu.

Many critter sports, such as camel racing and sheep dog trials, have evolved from the kind of work animals do.

As the roles of animals change, new sports will emerge from their new jobs. Sleeping by the TV and passing gas may become a new competitive sport for dogs. I once had a dog that could slobber half his own weight during a six-hour car ride. He rusted out the ashtrays in my Buick. There should be a competition for cross-country canine drooling. For cats, the hairball toss is a natural.

Donkey basketball is my favorite Extremely Dumb critter sport. It's usually played in a small town as a charity fundraiser, between two local teams such as the Lions and the Rotarians. Besides being enormously entertaining, donkey basketball demands wrangling skills not required in the NBA. I think professional basketball could benefit greatly by conversion to donkey ball.

Of course, the number of NBA games might be limited by the ASPCA. The donkeys would have to join a union, perhaps the Teamsters. They have horses on the union logo, so they must like animals. The donkeys would hire agents to set up endorsements. Best of all, it would no longer make the news when a pro athlete makes an ass of himself in public.

SLED DOG

"FETCH!"

RIDING LAWNMOWER

PET WARS

TROLLING FOR MOUNTAIN LIONS

It Takes Two to Tango

Prairie Dog Watching…A Popular Tourist Activity Out West

New Age Angst: Jeffrey Discovers His "Totem Animal"

DOUBLE DATE

GRIZZLY BEAR ARTIFICIAL-INSEMINATION TEAM

SEWER ROTTS--SCOURGE OF THE 'BURBS

Hunting and Fishing

Fishing and hunting celebrate the oldest of human endeavors. Early Man was drawn out of his cave to obtain food and clothing for his family (and to get away from Early Woman, who was always after him to help rearrange the boulders in the cave). Hunting got our species through the Ice Age. The fare must have become monotonous at times: "Mastodon for dinner again? Man, I'd kill for a salad!"

Fishing added variety to the Pleistocene diet, and afforded a level of frustration otherwise unachievable prior to the invention of golf.

Today, hunting is a recreational sport, a way to experience some of the distant, wild past without the extreme personal danger found in, say, biker bars. It's a way to reconnect with the natural world, and a great excuse for hanging around the woods drinking whiskey, eating pork rinds, and not bathing.

Hunting is becoming more diverse. People used to hunt with rifles or shotguns. Now they've added a season for black-powder muzzle-loading rifles, cross-bow season, bow season, atylatl season, spear season, and sticks and rocks season. Slingshots are fun, but don't use them on moose. It just pisses them off.

Fishing is the only good reason to get up before 5 a.m. (other than a raid from the DEA). There are two versions of this sport, fishing and angling. It's important to know the difference.

An angler arrives at the river or lake in a foreign car or SUV worth more than a modest home. He or she wears chest waders made from materials developed for NASA. His designer vest is organized to store all the tools and materials he needs, in alphabetical order. His hat doubles as a solar-powered navigation center, and his sunglasses are polarized to see through water, wood, and sand...anything but lead. He carries a hand-made graphite-fiber fly rod insured by Lloyd's of London.

A fisherman (or fisherperson) shows up in a beat-up Ford with primer on two fenders. He wears jeans and old sneakers and carries his fishing junk and lunch in a backpack or toolbox. He uses a rod and reel he bought on clearance at K Mart.

An angler believes that fishing with anything other than a microscopic dry fly (that he tied himself) is akin to using dynamite. A fisherman uses spoons, spinners, streamers, plugs, marshmallows, corn, live bait, or anything else that is legal and likely to catch fish. An angler releases her catch with a pat on the head and a stern lecture. She knows CPR in case a fish is too shocked by the experience to swim away. A fisherman knows how to release a fish, but also knows some great trout and bass recipes.

An angler can quote passages by Izaak Walton from memory. A fisherman can quote dirty limericks from memory. Angling is an art and a respected sport. Fishing is probably a sport, but it's more fun when one considers it a vice.

We who hunt and fish see nothing odd about staring into a hole in the ice for hours, or getting up at 4 a.m. on a cold day to hide in a duck blind. Hunting and fishing are considered Extremely Dumb Sports, mainly by people who don't hunt or fish (but what do they know?)

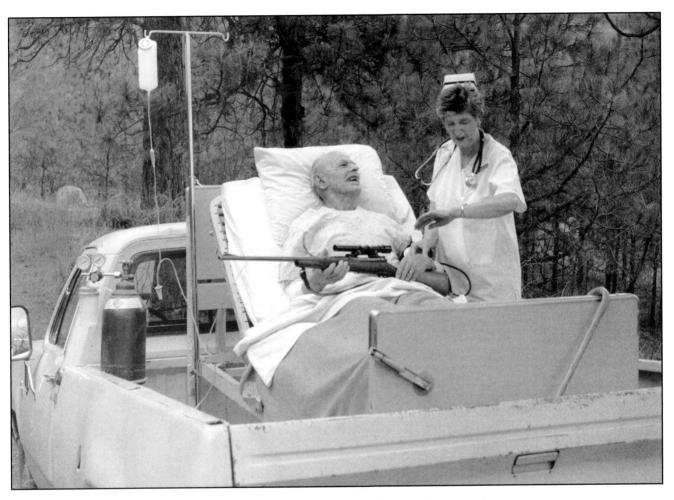

"MAYBE THIS IS THE LAST YEAR I'M GOIN' HUNTING"

GOOD HUNTING, BAD TIMING

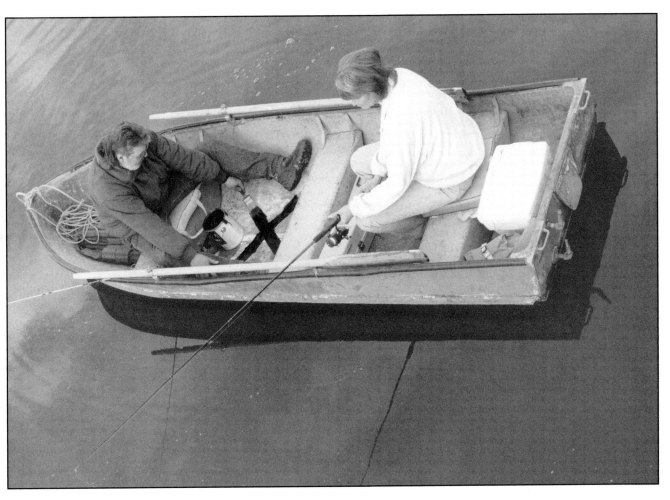

MYRON MARKS HIS FAVORITE FISHING SPOT

Blanche: "Myron, you idiot! What if we get a different boat next time?"

Wayne and Rodney's Mobile Duck Blind

Rᴇx ᴀɴᴅ Bᴏʙ Gᴏ Fɪsʜɪɴɢ

"GOIN' AFTER THE BIG ONE, AL?"

THE MORNING AFTER THE LAST DAY OF ELK SEASON

EXTREME ICE FISHING

Tourists Pay Big Bucks to Go Fishing for Sand Trout

Surviving Hunting Season

CATCH AND RELEASE FISHING

Training a Bird Dog

LARRY AND EARL'S NEW FISHFINDER

Winter Sports

The end of autumn doesn't reduce the number of stupid and dangerous activities available to the avid sports buff. Winter is like any other season, except cold, hard, and slippery. In northern states, the first snowfall brings the thrill of watching new emigrants from California or Florida skidding out of control through intersections.

As the mountains cover with snow, the skiers and snowboarders begin a vertical demolition derby. A snowboarder is like a skier who ends every declarative sentence with the word "dude." Cross-country skiing is also popular, and features the added perks of frostbite and avalanches.

Snowmobiling is a blue-collar sport, the winter equivalent of NASCAR. Unlike skiers, snowmobilers don't throw around French or German words (except *Bombardier* or *Budweiser*). A snowmobile is a sled propelled by smoke and noise. It's Middle America's closest thing to space flight. Snowmobilers dress in insulated moon suits and space helmets. They execute maneuvers that pull more G's than the centrifuge at Johnson Space Center.

My father introduced me to winter sports one Christmas morning in the 1950's with the gift of a shiny new Flexible Flyer sled. At the bottom of a long hill I learned that the "Flexible" part referred to the way the runner could wrap neatly around my neck.

That began my love for the Extremely Dumb Sport of sledding. My answer to equipment problems was to build my own larger, heavier, faster sled, which my friends called the "death sled." After several near-death experiences on Willow Creek Road, I installed brakes as an afterthought. One tip...never brake while crossing a cattle guard.

My sledding buddies and I could never understand the appeal of the Olympic version of the sport. In an Olympic bobsled, you run a fast, banked course in the company of people who know exactly what they're doing. The run is clear of other vehicles. You'll never come around a corner and meet some idiot who'll throw his 4X4 pickup into a sideways slide at first sight of you. Where's the fun in that?

My latest Extremely Dumb winter sport is snowkiting, which is to ski on a frozen, windswept lake attached to a very large kite. The kite can move me upwind at a good clip, downwind at mach II, or (unintentionally) airborne for entirely too far. It's a sport that allows you to get as beat-up as in downhill skiing, without paying for lift tickets. Recently I learned the hard way why almost everyone else in that sport is thirty years younger than I am. My fellow snowkiter's advice was, "Like, get some body armor, Dude."

"NEXT TIME, REMEMBER TO SHIFT YOUR WEIGHT"

WINTER CARPOOL

Proving that "male bonding" is overrated

THE ANNUAL MEETING OF "MONTANANS FOR GLOBAL WARMING"

HOME GROWN SKI RACK

WINTER DRAG RACING

THE MOOSE CREEK UPHILL BOBSLED TEAM

The Duckboy Interview:

The Moose Creek Uphill Bobsled Team

On March 16, 2003, Duckboy interviewed the members of the Moose Creek Uphill Bobsled Team, a group of four intrepid athletes hoping to see this rare and dangerous sport become an Olympic event. They are: team captain Buck Engelson, Dave Slomski, Charlie Sperry, and brakeman Bob Lemming. We spoke on a mountainside just north of Polaris, Montana, as the team prepared for a practice run.

Duckboy: Buck, everyone has heard of the four-man bobsled event, but your sport, uphill bobsledding, is relatively unknown. What is the difference, and what drew you to the sport?

Buck: I guess it was the challenge that attracted me. Anyone can get on a sled or skis and slide *down* a mountain. It's hard not to. But try going *up*. That's the tough part. Some of our equipment resembles downhill-bobsled gear, but we go in the opposite direction. Our sled is made of wood, from old shipping pallets, with a steel rack on the rear, to which we strap 8 or 9 oversized skyrockets. We get 'em from a fireworks factory in New Jersey. The rockets allow us to go up the hill instead of down.

Duckboy: Buck, how do you drive the sled?

Buck: Well, the front runners pivot, and I turn them by pushing on a steering bar with my feet, kind of like a kid's Flexible Flyer. There's no steering wheel. We don't have a prepared track. We just head uphill through the timber, and I try to steer around things. Dave sits behind me with a USGS topographic map, and tries to guide me, but it's not easy. Nobody can read a map that fast.

We have a safety device. Here in front we bolt part of the bumper from a '52 DeSoto. If we hit a boulder, or a log, or a moose, the sled will usually stop with little or no damage. But *we* usually keep going for a ways. That's when I'm glad not to have a steering wheel sticking up between my legs.

Duckboy: What sort of advance planning do you need to do?

Buck: The most important part is matching your rocket load to the mountain. You want enough push to make it to the top and no further. So it's important to know the height of the mountain exactly. One team in Colorado a few years ago used an old map that listed the hill at 11,921 feet, when it was really 11,291 feet.

Duckboy: What happened?

Buck: If a ski lodge hadn't got in the way, they might have won the uphill *and* downhill-bobsled competitions.

Duckboy: The idea of using fireworks rockets seems old-fashioned, somehow. Have you thought of using modern chemical rockets, like they use in the military?

Dave: One team from Idaho tried that. Somewhere they got ahold of some surplus surface-to-air missile engines.

Duckboy: How did that work?

Dave: Real effective. If you look at about eleven o'clock any clear night, just to the right of the Big Dipper, you should see 'em pass over.

Duckboy: You're hoping to see this become an Olympic event?

Buck: That's right. But it's a challenge to put together enough teams to pull it off. There's a big turnover in the sport.

Duckboy: This sounds like a dangerous sport, a sport for thrill-seekers. I'm wondering...what other kinds of activities do you guys enjoy?

Buck: We've all come to uphill bobsled from other extreme sports, things like boulder surfing, body bowling, whitewater hockey. Charlie, here, even drove a car in Boston once.

Duckboy: You guys really do live on the edge! I want to ask Bob Lemming, Bob, what is your job, as the team's brakeman?

Bob: I have several jobs. With the other guys, I have to lean into the turns. I operate the brakes, of course, but before the brakes will do any good, I have to use this bucket to scoop up snow and throw it into the rear of the rockets. I think that's where the expression "cool your jets" came from. I also light the fuses with a flare, like this here....

As Bob demonstrated his technique for lighting the fuses, sending this reporter diving for cover, the interview ended abruptly. The bobsled, belching smoke and fire, went whipsawing through the timber toward the summit of Mt. Tweedy, its valiant crew clinging to their bellowing chimera.

"I thought Stuart was spelled with a *W*"

SNOWSHOE BALLET

The Cowboy Way

Cowboy Sports grew out of the vaquero's regular working life on the range. He had to know how to handle large animals, cook over an open fire, milk a wild cow, and digest large quantities of beans without stampeding the herd.

The Cowboy Way celebrates a noble tradition of hard work and fair play. It's real men in high heels, and women who wear spurs.

Rodeo is probably the most honest of all animal sports, because it's the only one where you *assume* the animal wants to kill you. It's a link to the time when humans first tried to domesticate wild beasts.

We have to marvel at the first proto-cowboy, who saw a wild horse and thought, "There's an ill-tempered 1,400-lb creature with big teeth and four sharp hooves. I think I'll go climb on its back!"

Horse riding may be Extremely Dumb, but it's eminently sensible compared to climbing onto a large bull or steer. This is an animal fully aware of its destiny (inside a Big Mac) and that doesn't help its disposition.

At some time, almost everyone wants to be a cowboy or a cowgirl. Of course, many people who wear pointy boots and blue jeans are just dressing the part... "All hat and no cattle," as they say around here.

Sometimes a young fellow goes Out West and decides it might be fun to ask a cowgirl for a date. The dude forgets, or doesn't know, the *Three Rules for Dating a Cowgirl*:

1. Watch out for spurs.

2. Don't kiss her until you check for snoose.

3. Unless you want to be roped and branded, show some respect.

While the Cowboy Way helps preserve the flavor of the Old West, it also proves that Extremely Dumb Sports aren't limited to city slickers.

Proto-Cowboy

SUNDAY MORNING: SWEARING OFF COWGIRLS FOR THE 87TH TIME

NEVER DISRESPECT A COWGIRL

COWBOY SKEET SHOOTING

DESIGNATED DRIVER

STRETCH McCOY, FAMOUS TRAIN ROPER

COWBOY DRIVING RANGE

Texas Tea Bag

Vegetarian Cowboys

COWGIRL DENTAL FLOSS

FLOYD TRIES TO GO ON LINE

"COULDN'T YOU GET THE GUY WITH THE HARMONICA?"

THE TROUBLE WITH A SHORT HORSE

IDAHO'S OLYMPIC FENCING TEAM

Panning for Plutonium

The Active Lifestyle

The world of sports isn't the only opportunity to engage in stupid and dangerous activities. Sometimes real life can be almost as weird as the sports we're able to invent. Depending on how you live it, life itself can be an Extremely Dumb Sport.

Buying a home can be a horrifying ordeal. You never really know when your realtor is a Master of the Dark Arts. Computer viruses can enter your home's wiring and cause your appliances to mutiny.

These days, you can't even own an acre or two of wrecked automobiles without the government conspiring against you. As an urban refugee hiding out in a cabin in the Montana backwoods recently ranted, "The price of freedom isn't vigilance, it's paranoia!"

Going to the hairdresser or talking on a cell phone can be a grueling contest in the sport of living. Just getting by is often the toughest competition. To demonstrate this, I've included a few photos of events that are outside the conventional realm of sports, but uphold the proud tradition of Extreme Dumbness.

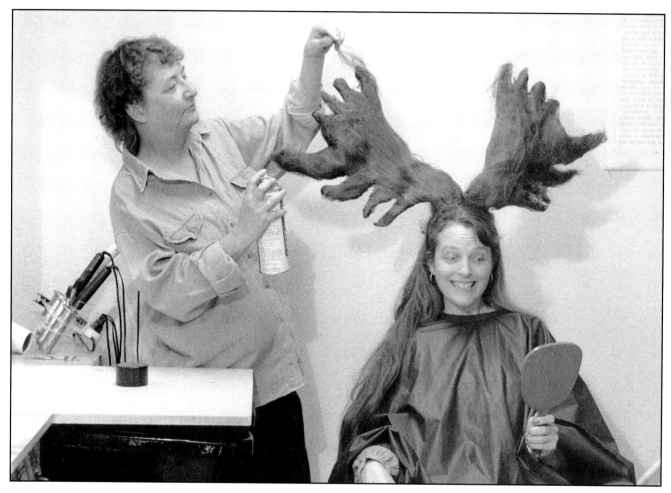

GETTING HER HAIR MOOSED

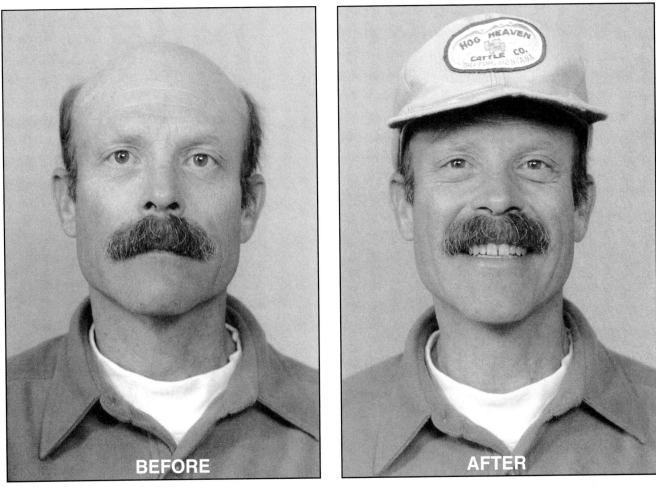

BEFORE

AFTER

AMERICA'S FAVORITE HAIRPIECE

TRUCK FARMING

TIFFANY LOVES HER NEW CELLPHONE IMPLANT

THE DARK SIDE OF TECHNOLOGY

HIGH NOON IN THE NEW WEST

"I'D BETTER CALL YOU BACK"

WHERE JERKY COMES FROM

"Them ain't indoor chickens, Clyde. Them's *free range* Chickens"

"YOU GOT YOUR ARIZONA RETIREMENT HOME. NOW WHAT'S WRONG?"

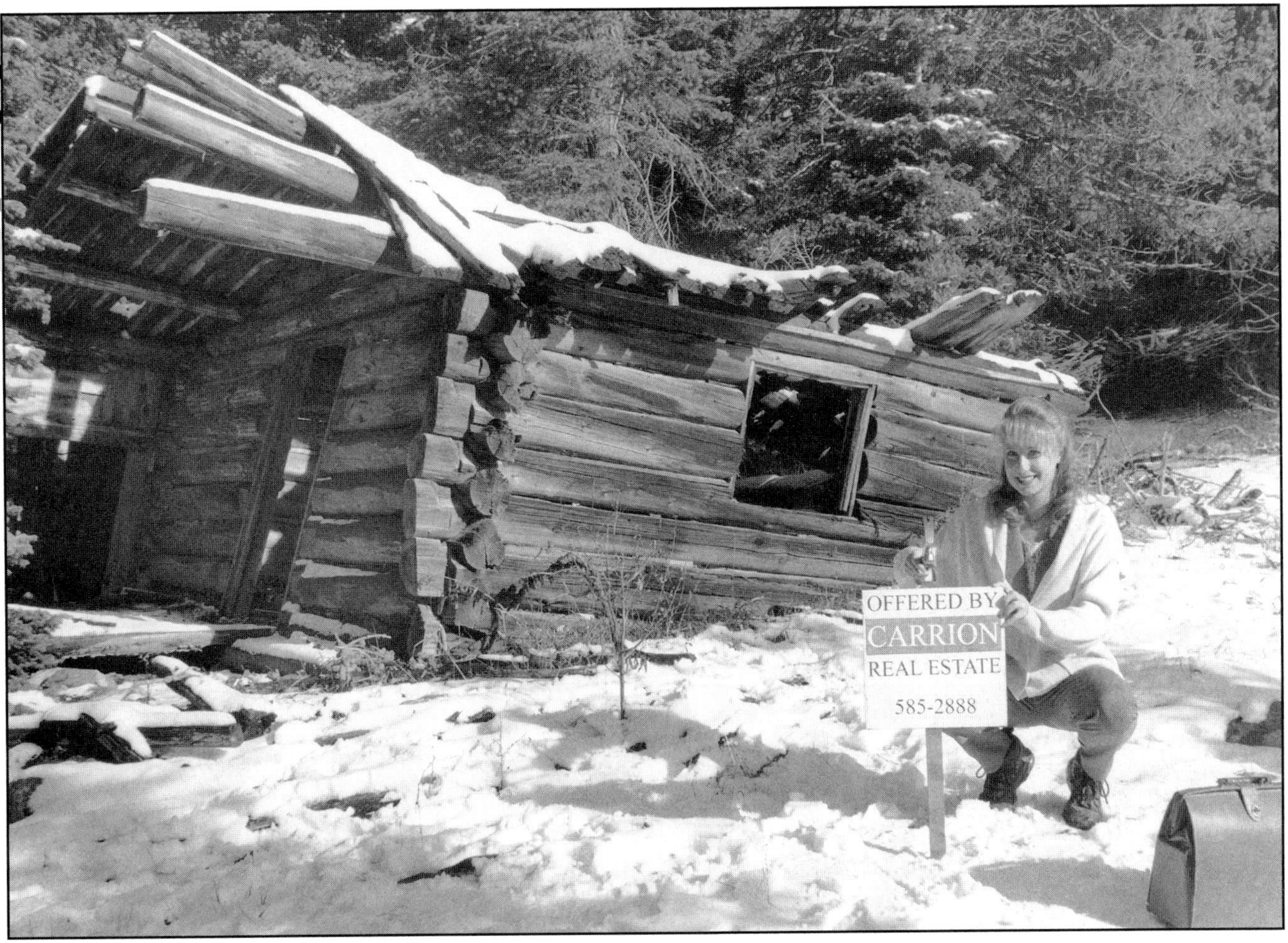
OFFERED BY
CARRION
REAL ESTATE
585-2888

Handyman Special

LAND USE PLANNING

WINE TASTING IN CALIFORNIA

THE DUCKBOY THINK TANK